Austin has long beckoned creative souls, musicians and offbeat misfits. But in the past few years, its appeal has extended to techies, indie filmmakers and foodies, too. It's a mix that elsewhere might struggle to find common ground – not so in Austin.

A blend of Southern hospitality and earthy crunchiness imbues the air here, making the locals friendly and the city eco-conscious. Despite tremendous growth over the last half-decade, Austin is still a land of craggy creeks, shimmering lakes and natural springs – it's not uncommon, for example, to see stand-up paddlers moseying along Lake Austin at all hours of the day, or South Austinites taking their lunch break at Barton Springs.

"Hunting" in this city of delightful weirdos is effortless: there is always a fantastic band lighting up the night, or a newly opened restaurant luring you in by the nostrils. So consider this guide a collection of the most potent sources of wonder, by a local who is still discovering Austin's sunny, lovely corners.

the hunt austin editor

tolly moseley

Based in the gorgeous city of Austin, Texas, Tolly Moseley is a writer, aerial silks dancer and yoga teacher. All of which means that she spends half her time performing an array of bodily contortions and the other half hunched over a computer. Her work has appeared in *Salon*, *Texas Parks & Wildlife Magazine* and the *Austin American-Statesman*, and on National Public Radio Austin, as well as her parent's refrigerator. She tells stories about her life on her blog, austineavesdropper.com.

where to lay your weary head

Rest up, relax and recharge

HEYWOOD HOTEL

Crafted dwellings in Austin's hip East Side

1609 East Cesar Chavez (78702) / +1 512 271 5522 / heywoodhotel.com

Double from $219

Operated by husband and wife George Reynolds and Kathy Setzer, Heywood Hotel is home to seven uniquely designed, sleek rooms, each of which will make you feel like signing up for a long-term lease. Decorated with artwork from local Austin artists and outfitted with beds George made himself, Heywood possesses an atmosphere that feels at once artful and homey. It's also within walking distance of some of east Austin's coolest art studios, vintage stores and eateries.

HOTEL SAINT CECILIA

Rock 'n' roll luxury in a secluded forest

112 Academy Drive (78704) / +1 512 852 2400 / hotelsaintcecilia.com

Double from $340

On a sprawling property squirreled away in Austin's hilly 78704, Hotel Saint Cecilia will make you feel like rock-star royalty. Each of the 14 rooms is outfitted with turntables, iPod connections and a Geneva sound system, not to mention ultra-stylish décor. On top of that, their chevron-floored lounge looks nothing like a hotel bar – more like the amazing living room of a celebrity. One with fantastic taste, mind you.

HOTEL SAINT CECILIA

HOTEL SAN JOSÉ

Contemporary luxe, Zen garden surroundings

1316 South Congress Avenue (78704) / +1 512 444 7322 / sanjosehotel.com

Double from $205

If you like being in the middle of all the action but still crave a calm oasis, you can't do better than Hotel San José. The 40-room collection of minimalist urban bungalows faces directly out to bustling South Congress Avenue. For those who prefer something more chilled, there's also a wine bar downstairs in a modern, sleek courtyard.

KIMBER MODERN

Scandinavian modern in the South Congress neighborhood

110 The Circle (78704) / +1 512 912 1046 / kimbermodern.com

Double from $265

In the tradition of HomeAway and Vacation Rentals By Owner (VRBO), this lobbyless hotel provides travelers a true feeling of autonomy: you receive your room code in advance, and then settle in to enjoy what feels like a stylish townhouse. Kimber Modern's architecturally striking, white and clean lines reach up into a canopy of trees that makes their second-story deck and window-walled common area feel both polished and nature-filled.

THE DRISKILL

Handsome Texan finery that may or may not be haunted

604 Brazos Street (78701) / +1 512 439 1234 / driskillhotel.com

Double from $299

Grand and richly historic, The Driskill is perfect for anyone who not only needs to be downtown but also wants a big ol' taste of Texas. The majestic lobby here is equal parts glittering chandeliers and longhorn paintings, and is usually filled with senators and big-wigs milling about supping whiskey on the rocks. This is also an excellent choice for Halloween too, since The Driskill is widely rumored to be haunted.

downtown

market district, seaholm district

Both a business district and a party district, downtown Austin is the ultimate happy hour destination: a place where you can't throw a rock without hitting a cocktail lounge or shot bar. It's also beautifully bordered by a large stretch of water and surrounding running trail, filled morning to night with the more virtuous among us. There's a couple of independent movie theaters here, too (try the Violet Crown if your tastes lean towards art house, see pg 20), along with fabulous dining and high-end shopping options. In particular, 2nd Street is lined with pretty boutiques designed to crack even the tightest of wallets, as I can personally attest.

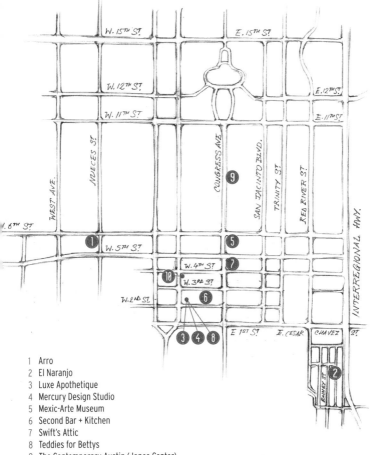

1 Arro
2 El Naranjo
3 Luxe Apothetique
4 Mercury Design Studio
5 Mexic-Arte Museum
6 Second Bar + Kitchen
7 Swift's Attic
8 Teddies for Bettys
9 The Contemporary Austin (Jones Center)
10 TRACE

ARRO

Luscious, non-intimidating French fare

601 West 6th Street (78701) / +1 512 992 2776 / arroaustin.com
Open daily

Housed in a bright, window-wrapped corner of 6th Street, Arro features a menu that makes unfussy family-style dining incredibly fun. The seafood stew is a nice place to start, and even if you share it with a friend, you'll want to slurp up its gorgeous fennel, tomato and leek broth all by yourself. The coup de grâce, though, is the dessert menu: the cookie plate, for example, is full of elegant details (black lava salt on the chocolate chip cookies, olive oil in the shortbread). And in case you don't, make somebody at your table order the lemon goat cheese tart. None of you will be sorry.

EL NARANJO

Elevated Mexican cuisine

85 Rainey Street (78701) / +1 512 474 2776 / elnaranjo-restaurant.com
Closed Monday

Don't mistake El Naranjo for just another Tex-Mex hangout. Chef Iliana de la Vega draws on her Oaxacan roots to craft exceptionally good traditional dishes, with tangy, flavor-layered sauces, bright vegetables and serious proteins (duck, buttery sea bass, sushi grade ahi tuna). There's very little flour used in the kitchen, making most of the menu naturally gluten-free. Except, that is, for the ciabatta rolls handmade by Iliana's daughter each morning, and the terribly good Mexican sweet rolls she bakes on weekends.

LUXE APOTHETIQUE

Downtown boutique with in-house apothecary

201 West 2nd Street (78758) / +1 512 215 0282
luxeapothetique.tumblr.com / Open daily

Austin's 2nd Street is home to a lot of great fashion retailers, but Luxe Apothetique is particularly lovely in that it's equal opportunity shopping: there's the high-end (Marc by Marc Jacobs) and the mid-level (Roxy), with a mish-mash of boho chic and sparkly party gear. In addition, they specialize in cute (not cheesy) Austin souvenirs, as well as quality beauty products (Kerastase, Bumble and bumble) and a whole slew of nail polishes. Ah, and did I mention the free wine and cookies while you shop?

MERCURY DESIGN STUDIO

All things bright and beautiful

209 West 2nd Street (78701) / +1 512 236 0100
mercurydesignstudio.com / Open daily

Mercury Design Studio is one of those places where anyone with a smart phone and a Pinterest account would have a field day. Impeccably put together and packed with artsy objects, it's a gift shop/home furnishings boutique that is "full of moments", as owner Steve Shuck says. He's right: there's an unfinished table adorned with Victorian plates here, a wooden hand holding beaded neck plates there, all surrounded by slate-gray walls covered with interesting, obscure art. Part Etsy, part vintage, part discoveries from every corner of the globe, Mercury Design Studio is like the weird kid sister to Anthropologie: less precious, but equally covetable.

MEXIC-ARTE MUSEUM

Vibrant Latin American art

419 Congress Avenue (78701) / +1 512 480 9373
mexic-artemuseum.org / Open daily

Artistic innovation exists all over the city, but one of my favorite places sits on a bustling corner of downtown Austin smack dab in the middle of a business district: Mexic-Arte Museum. Not only does Mexic-Arte foster the wide talents of Texas' Latino art community, it features work from Latino artists across the U.S., Mexico and Central/South America. At any time of year, you'll find evocative work that draws on the themes of cultural experience: the mysticism of death around Día de los Muertos, vintage Mexican cinema posters and Central American political cartoons. The gift shop is also terrific, packed as it is with colorful wares and pieces for the home.

SECOND BAR + KITCHEN

American staples with a high-end twist

200 Congress Avenue (78701) / +1 512 827 2750
congressaustin.com/second / Open daily

Parked in an industrial modern space at a busy intersection, Second Bar + Kitchen boasts a big, confident menu that ranges from gourmet bar food (buffalo fried pickles) to fancy-pants pizza such as "the black and bleu", black referring to truffles and bleu to cheese, hitched deliciously together by pork belly and dates. Chef David Bull cut his teeth on *Iron Chef America* and the CIA (the Culinary Institute of America, not the other CIA), and has been recognized by the likes of James Beard and *Food & Wine Magazine*.

SWIFT'S ATTIC

Dazzling dishes and decor

315 Congress Avenue (78701) / +1 512 482 8842
swiftsattic.com / Open daily

This pleasantly raucous eatery serves up some downright ravishing dishes that – small and tapas-like as they are – encourage one to experiment fearlessly. The warm Nieman pork cheeks are a popular staple on the ever-evolving menu: they arrive in a little sandwich-making kit alongside spicy mustard, fig preserves and warm sourdough toast. You always hear "leave room for dessert" – but in this case it really is crucial, because you don't want to leave without tasting one of pastry chef Callie Speer's creations. Proof? Order "Popcorn & a Movie", an upscale play on movie munchies involving butter popcorn gelato, candy bars and root beer gel.

TEDDIES FOR BETTYS

Hot lingerie

221 West 2nd Street (78701) / +1 512 614 2103 / teddiesforbettys.com
Open daily

Be they everyday underthings or once-in-a-while unmentionables, Teddies for Bettys is the go-to shop for luxe lingerie. Granted, items purchased here are an investment, but every agent provocateur enjoys having a few fancy tricks up her sleeve, no? The merchandise on display will provide plenty of those, but also check out the drawers underneath for a broader selection: Teddies carries a fantastic variety of sizes, including maternity lines. Everything here is made out of the good stuff, and is so comfy on, it feels like a second skin.

THE CONTEMPORARY AUSTIN (JONES CENTER)

Downtown art epicenter

700 Congress Avenue (78701) / **+1 512 453 5312**
thecontemporaryaustin.org / **Closed Monday**

Austin hasn't always been a mecca for contemporary art. Our Texas city brethren Dallas and Houston are the ones with more museums, more patrons, more of a reputation. Until, that is, The Contemporary Austin launched a bold new vision in 2013: to combine two local art spaces (Arthouse at the Jones Center and Austin Museum of Art – Laguna Gloria, see pg 98) under one compelling name, and began exhibiting work by today's leading artists. You'll find provocative multimedia work, from large-scale sculpture to video, and site-specific installations that immerse the viewer in a full-sensory experience. Besides visuals, artists here have also made clever use of music, performance and even fragrance for their shows

TRACE

Fancy local produce and foraged food

200 Lavaca Street (78701) / +1 512 542 3660 / traceaustin.com
Open daily

TRACE at the W Austin Hotel defies any preconceived notion you may have of the hotel dining experience. Growing much of their own food on the building's roof and procuring the rest from local farms and their on-staff forager (officially the coolest job ever), TRACE's cuisine isn't just hyper-local, it's hyper, period. Chefs here craft imaginative plates and desserts, like the famous Drunken Donuts that comes with chili fudge sauce and bourbon dulce de leche. And while we're on the subject of hotel restaurants, let's discuss décor: TRACE's is the opposite of dowdy, with enormous, airy windows, modern gray touches and fabrics you just know made an interior designer squeal.

ALAMO DRAFTHOUSES
Various locations, drafthouse.com/austin, open daily

HIDEOUT THEATRE
617 Congress Avenue (78701), +1 512 443 3688
hideouttheatre.com, opening subject to show times

THE PARAMOUNT THEATRE
713 Congress Avenue (78701), +1 512 472 5470, austintheatre.org
opening subject to show times

VIOLET CROWN CINEMA
434 West 2nd Street (78701), +1 512 495 9600
violetcrowncinema.com, open daily

ALAMO DRAFTHOUSE

stage and screen

Evening entertainment

Maybe it's Austin's legacy of indie filmmakers, or maybe it's the fact that we're extremely geeky, but either way, we locals love us some movies. Get in on the action at one of several local **Alamo Drafthouses**, which screen them in a fun way: you order drinks and food from your seat, and before your movie rolls, a hilarious, house-made reel of kitschy throwbacks and cartoons flashes across the screen. Alamo Drafthouse also hosts various sing-alongs (90's Pop Stars, for instance) and quote-alongs (*The Princess Bride* is a popular one).

Violet Crown Cinema is a bona fide art house, where you can catch foreign flicks and Cannes winners alike in comfy, first-class-flight-like seats that accommodate a glass of wine and classy appetizer.

During summertime, **The Paramount Theatre** – a grand old show house on Congress Avenue – operates a Summer Classic Film Series, screening favorites such as *Casablanca* and *Singin' in the Rain* on glorious 35mm.

And finally, if you dig improv, there's nowhere better than **Hideout Theatre**. My favorite is when they take a theme like Shakespeare or Woody Allen, and create on-the-spot plays that are wonderfully funny.

hyde park and campus

hancock

With historical roots in the 19th century and a close-knit, village vibe, Hyde Park – my first residence in Austin – will steal your heart instantly. Walkable and friendly, with a regular cast of characters who hang out at neighborhood coffee shops, it's a mostly residential area with small pockets of business: juice bars, family-owned restaurants and a curiously popular gas station covered in international flags. It neighbors the University of Texas at Austin (UT) campus area, a bustling scene bisected by Guadalupe Street ("The Drag"), its main cultural artery. Here you can find record shops, vintage stores and UT students either trudging to class or skipping off to parties – just remember to drop the "e" on Guadalupe (say: Guad-a-loop) to sound like a local.

1 Antonelli's Cheese Shop
2 Antone's Record Shop
3 ASTI Trattoria
4 FINO
5 Foreign & Domestic
6 Gallery Black Lagoon
7 Hopfields
8 Spider House Cafe

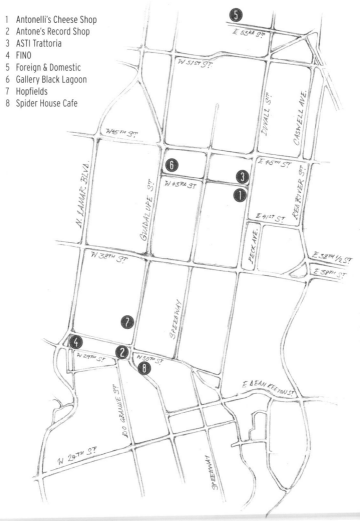

ANTONELLI'S CHEESE SHOP

Little wedges of dairy heaven

4220 Duval Street (78751) / +1 512 531 9610 / antonellischeese.com
Closed Monday

When Antonelli's first opened, my husband and I walked by it and jeered, "Seriously? A shop just devoted to cheese? Like that's going to last!" My, how wrong we were. Antonelli's, a sophisticated and petite dairy grocer, is quickly becoming a local institution: the place where both professional cheese mongers and novices go to school their palates. Tastings here are very fun, with selections ranging from buttery bries to grassy sheep wedges, so enter with an open mind and a sense of adventure. The friendly staff will know exactly where to point your tongue.

ANTONE'S RECORD SHOP

Vinyl treasure trove

2928 Guadalupe Street (78705) / +1 512 322 0660
antonesrecordshop.com / Open daily

A storied little music shop just steps away from the UT campus, this is the storefront baby of Clifford Antone, whose downtown rock and blues club (Antone's) helped put Austin on the national music map in the 1970s. As a result, blues is the beating heart of this record store, flanked by deep collections of jazz, surfer rock, a smattering of country and even local stuff. If you don't own a record player, Antone's is the kind of place that will make you desperately want one.

ASTI TRATTORIA

Contemporary Italian

408 East 43rd Street (78751) / +1 512 451 1218 / astiaustin.com
Closed Sunday

Cozy and stylish, ASTI is a couple-owned Italian eatery with an abiding affection for truffles. They appear on your pizza, in your vegetables, in the heady oil coating your salmon: this is rich stuff, so the portions are petite. Though various sous chefs have passed through ASTI's doors in its near decade-and-a-half history, the food here is always carefully rendered: the bianca pizza, for example, gets a flavor boost from fried sage (and, of course, truffle); warm beignets come with vanilla ice cream and espresso, the latter intended to pour into the former for a perfect affogato dipping sauce. This neighborhood spot's laid-back elegance is just right for a special occasion.

FINO

Mediterranean cuisine in unexpected digs

**2905 San Gabriel Street (78705) / +1 512 474 2905 / finoaustin.com
Open daily**

There's so much to say about FINO, a Mediterranean joint curiously perched on the second floor of an office park. But my favorite feature about this classy little spot is the paella (inhale, dramatic pause) happy hour. Every Tuesday from 5–7pm, FINO's succulent pans of paella are discounted by 50 per cent, and one order can easily satisfy two people. Selections change seasonally, but expect to find spicy chorizo, baby octopi, aioli-rich mussels and a slew of flavorful vegetables in your order, as well as a shallow layer of blackened rice that sticks crunchily, tantalizingly to the bottom of the pan.

FOREIGN & DOMESTIC

Neighborhood gourmet

306 East 53rd Street (78751) / +1 512 459 1010 / fndaustin.com
Closed Sunday and Monday

An upscale gastropub, Foreign & Domestic loves nothing more than to play with its food. Ned Elliott is the kind of chef who picks up various ingredients and wonders what sort of culinary alchemy he can perform. The result is an ever-changing, New American menu with offerings such as prosciutto and basil, peaches and goat cheese, roasted quail with duck tongue stew – I've even had brain (yep, brain) here once, which was shockingly tasty. A bonus: food at this level should make your wallet shrink back in horror, but here it needn't worry. Everything is priced reasonably enough to keep you coming back for more.

GALLERY BLACK LAGOON

Contemporary art and yoga

4301A Guadalupe Street (78751) / +1 512 534 6719
galleryblacklagoon.com / Open by appointment and viewing days

Gallery Black Lagoon has an exacting eye for provocative visual art, drawing work from local and national artists alike, across every medium: paintings, silkscreen, lithography, intaglio. What's more, they offer yoga, and it's probably not only me that finds yoga surrounded by art just about the coolest exercise you can get. Classes are held every day except Friday, and range from relaxing hatha to core strength vinyasa with some of the best rates in town: $10 for a drop-in class. There's also a pizza joint next door, where you can reward yourself for having burned all those calories.

HOPFIELDS

Cozy French gastropub

3110 Guadalupe Street (78705) / +1 512 537 0467
hopfieldsaustin.com / Open daily

Even though it's only been open since 2011, Hopfields feels like a home that's been in the family for years, with antique china and old photos scattered among contemporary trappings. The food is traditional French (think ratatouille, steak frites, luscious fruit crêpes) and the beverages are microbrew beers and fancy cocktails, making this a place for both bon vivants and renegade yogis. My favorite bit? The hidden nooks tucked inside Hopfields. There's a communal dining room in front, but as you walk down their dark hallway, you'll discover private little rooms, enclosed by fringe and low lighting.

SPIDER HOUSE CAFE

Eclectic coffee house, classic Austin

2906 Fruth Street (78705) / +1 512 480 9562 / spiderhousecafe.com
Open daily

With enough colored twinkly lights to outfit 20 Christmas trees and
random statues scattered about, Spider House Cafe is one part coffee
shop, one part art experiment. Its clutter is refreshing in a city of
increasingly curated spaces, whose restraint can feel more "Keep Austin
Cool" than "Keep Austin Weird". Those sparse rooms are nice too, but
Spider House recalls an Austin more defiantly freaky, which is probably
why it consistently attracts college kids from just up the road. In the
process themselves of liberating their inner freaks, this place feels like a
welcoming, eclectic safe haven, with late-night study food (chili-drenched
Frito burritos and warm, chocolatey brownies) aplenty.

cherrywood and mueller

On the north end of Austin's East Side, you'll find Mueller and Cherrywood, two neighborhoods with distinctive, yet complementary, personalities. The site of recent commercial development, Mueller was built on the grounds of Austin's old airport, Robert Mueller Municipal Airport, whose Browning Hangar still stands (only now it houses farmers' markets instead of airplanes). Next door to Mueller, Cherrywood marks the start of your journey into east Austin proper, and what a tasty journey it is. Manor Road is sprinkled with hip eateries tucked into demure bungalows, hidden food trailers, and former pizza joints. Come with an appetite.

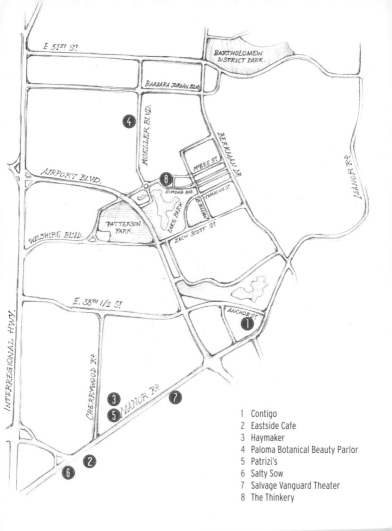

1 Contigo
2 Eastside Cafe
3 Haymaker
4 Paloma Botanical Beauty Parlor
5 Patrizi's
6 Salty Sow
7 Salvage Vanguard Theater
8 The Thinkery

CONTIGO

Hill Country eating, gourmand cooking

**2027 Anchor Lane (78723) / +1 512 614 2260 / contigotexas.com
Open daily**

Dinner at Contigo is a bit like dining at a flinty Texas ranch, only with a gourmet chef in the kitchen rather than Uncle Steve sipping a Bud Light. Though the menu is haute Hill Country, the (all outdoor) atmosphere is kid- and dog-friendly, which makes for a relaxed feel. Food selections change daily, but you'll usually find Texas game (quail, rabbit) and some truly creative elements (bacon jam, anyone?). The secret to this seasonal kitchen is Southern and Texan classics (pigs in a blanket, fried okra), but with international twists: a little miso here, some bordelaise there. It's a darn tasty melting pot.

EASTSIDE CAFE

From-the-farm comfort food

2113 Manor Road (78722) / +1 512 476 5858
eastsidecafeaustin.com / Open daily

There's meatloaf, and then there's meatloaf doused in tangy, Shiner Bock tomato sauce, laced with bacon and chunky with vegetables. Eating at Eastside Cafe is like sitting down to a meal prepared by your most kitchen-savvy pal, in a homespun house with a garden out back and some Otis Redding hits playing in the background. The food here is fresh, farm-grown comfort, with many of your meal's herbs and greens picked that day, and your brunch eggs laid by the feathered friends you'll see roaming the property.

HAYMAKER

Pro-dude Midwestern grub

**2310 Manor Road (78722) / +1 512 243 6702 / haymakeraustin.com
Open daily**

Some restaurants in Austin are known for crafting shrewd, tiny bites of pleasure, layering each sprig of green against each morsel of caviar just so. Haymaker is not one of them. Instead, this Midwest-inspired bar and eatery is known for big, badass nosh, where cheese is a huge deal. So much so, that curds are couriered overnight from Wisconsin to the kitchen where they are put to genius use. The Louisville Slugger gleefully smothers thick bacon, tomato and roasted turkey breast with gruyère sauce and parmesan, while the classic Fluffenutty Cristo (peanut butter and marshmallow crème on white bread) is a whopping favorite.

PALOMA BOTANICAL BEAUTY PARLOR

Quirky art gallery-cum-beauty salon

4600 Mueller Boulevard (78723) / +1 512 480 8090
palomabeauty.com / Closed Monday, appointment only

I walked into Paloma a few years ago, intrigued by a little care package they had sent me. Facials used to make me nervous, but that fateful day turned me into a believer. Co-owner Evette Richards bathed my face with organics, and a few peels later, I left with the prettiest pallor I've ever had. I returned for a haircut. Then a massage. Then an art opening. It's now gotten to the point where I'm at this boutique-cum-beauty parlor every other week, and who can blame me? With heavenly services and killer interior design it's an easy place to while away the better part of an afternoon.

PATRIZI'S

Homemade Italian from a trailer

2307 Manor Road (78722) / +1 512 814 8579 / patrizis.com
Open daily

When it comes to a regular location, food trailers can be fickle, but Italian Patrizi's is one I'd deem worthy of chasing down should it ever uproot to a new spot. The homemade pasta is cooked to order, and the ricotta made daily; in fact, so much of the food here is either local, organic or coddled into being by the chef's own hands that the "trailer" part is incidental — this is some of the best Italian in town. And if you fancy rounding off your meal with a nice wine, you won't have to go far — just pop to the nearby Butterfly Bar.

SALTY SOW

Nose-to-tail farmhouse cuisine

1917 Manor Road (78722) / +1 512 391 2337 / saltysow.com
Open daily

Head-to-tail dining might not be for everyone, but Salty Sow is capable
of bringing even the most dogged vegan to their knees. Though the
menu changes daily, you can expect to find variations on pork belly, slick
with gristle and ultra-soft; a duck dish (triple fried duck-fat fries, if you're
lucky), and some animal's shoulder or thighs (the former usually a cow's,
braised to glisten; the latter typically a chicken's and crisped just right).
But a surprising standout at this outstanding establishment? The brussels
sprouts: leafed, flash fried in olive oil and topped with pecorino. The rich
smell alone is many an Austinite's favorite sense memory.

SALVAGE VANGUARD THEATER

Wry, evocative productions

2803 Manor Road (78722) / +1 512 474 7886 / salvagevanguard.org
Opening subject to show times

Though overshadowed by its more famous cultural counterpart, live music, Austin's simmering theater scene is both talent-filled and ripe with date-night potential – especially if you and your partner have a taste for the offbeat. Salvage Vanguard Theater offers some of the weirdest, most fantastic stuff, especially if you go during FronteraFest (mid-January through mid-February), when you can catch puppet shows, faux lecture tours, comedy, cabaret, or full plays by both emerging and established playwrights. Manor Road is downright messy with great restaurants, too (several of which appear in this chapter), for

THE THINKERY

Where learning is fun

1830 Simond Avenue (78723) / +1 512 469 6200 / thinkeryaustin.org
Closed Monday

When I was a little girl, my mom used to take me to the Children's Museum in downtown Austin – a colorful, whimsical place with prop-filled rooms and learning stations. My favorite activity back then was pretend grocery shopping, where children measured out their bulk items with mini scoopers and weighed them for "purchase" (is it any wonder I still love the bulk section?). Reopened as The Thinkery, the museum is now designed for the 21st-century kiddo, with a physics-like "Innovation Station", a mock cafeteria, a splash zone and two stories of other sensory delights. Bring your little ones and let the exploration begin.

best barbecue

Where carnivores get their fix.

FRANKLIN BARBECUE
900 East 11th Street (78702), +1 512 653 1187, franklinbarbecue.com
lunch only, closed Monday

JOHN MUELLER MEAT CO.
2500 East 6th Street (78702), +1 512 524 0559
johnmuellermeatco.com, closed Wednesday

LA BARBECUE
1200 East 6th Street (78702), +1 512 605 9696, labarbecue.com
closed Monday and Tuesday

LIVE OAK BARBECUE
2713 East 2nd Street (78702), +1 512 524 1930, liveoakbbq.net
open daily

MICKLETHWAIT CRAFT MEATS
1309 Rosewood Avenue (78702), +1 512 791 5961, craftmeats.com
closed Monday and Tuesday

THE BLUE OX BBQ
1505 Town Creek Drive (78741), +1 512 537 2047
blueoxbarbecue.com, lunch only, open daily

THE SALT LICK
18300 FM 1826, Driftwood (78619), +1 512 894 3117, saltlickbbq.com
open daily

LIVE OAK BARBECUE

Austin may be Texas' number one hippie enclave, equally attracted to buckwheat as we are to brisket, but that doesn't mean we fall short in the barbecue department. In fact **Franklin Barbecue**, currently the most famous and most popular grill in these parts, was declared the "best BBQ in America" by *Bon Appétit* magazine. That's right: America. Their tender slabs of meat, covered in barbecue sauce shot through with espresso, certainly warrant the praise.

If the lines at Franklin Barbecue are too much for you, head up the road to **Live Oak Barbecue**, whose nondescript exterior belies the artsy handling of meat within. On Saturdays, Tom the Pitmaster whips up fantastic off-menu specials such as duck tamales, beef short ribs with apple wasabi sauce and pork belly confit with green chile mustard. Also on the East Side is **Micklethwait Craft Meats**, a trailer that cranks out some seriously outstanding sausages (duck and fig, for example), not to mention spicy jalapêno cheese grits. **La Barbecue** is a few blocks away, and the brisket – smoked for almost an entire day – almost needs no sauce, the naked flavor is so good. You could also skip right over to **John Mueller Meat Co**. Meat here is seasoned with just the right amount of spice and, judging by his gloriously peppered ribs, Mueller's salty mouth barks out perfect smoker instructions. In a different corner of east Austin lies **The Blue Ox BBQ**, a trailer parked right behind Buzz Mill Coffee, and here I would recommend anything involving pork: the pulled pork sandwich is huge, moist and tangily sweet, while the espresso-rubbed pork tenderloin deftly avoids the dryness some tenderloins acquire, coming out instead perfectly juicy.

It's here that you can emerge from the East Side and head south, all the way down to Driftwood, just outside of Austin city limits. **The Salt Lick** stands alone in a field of centuries-old trees, girded by a winery and an absolutely huge open pit: this is where your dinner shall be prepared, over clean-burning live oak. Each piece of meat falls deliciously apart with smoky flavor, illustrating immediately why this is one of the most beloved Texas barbecue joints of all.

the east side

There's a crackling, electric energy that seems
to pervade east Austin and in truth, this
neighborhood has always had a vibrant cultural
scene – B.B. King used to play on East 11th Street
at the Victory Grill, along with Billie Holiday
and James Brown in the 1950s. In the past few
decades, an enormous influx of new culinary and
artistic talent has taken up residence here as well.
You could easily spend a day just eating your way
through hip cafés, and in November of each year,
the area's artists open up their homes and studios
for my favorite event on the Austin calendar:
East Austin Studio Tour (pg 60).

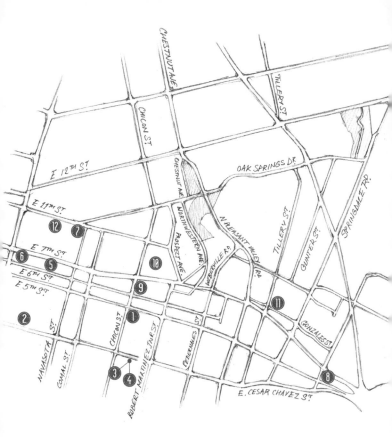

1 Busy Being / Solid Gold
2 Cazamance Cafe
3 Charm School Vintage
4 Coco Coquette
5 East Side Show Room
6 HELM Boots

7 Hillside Farmacy
8 Justine's Brasserie
9 qui
10 Salt & Time
11 Swoop House
12 Take Heart

BUSY BEING/SOLID GOLD

Classy boutique meets artful gift shop

**1601 East 5th Street (78702) / +1 512 473 2730 / busy-being.com,
solidgoldacademy.com / Open daily**

This is a glorious marriage between Solid Gold and Busy Being, the former
a curated clothing boutique, the latter a peddler of interesting objects.
Here, you can find a choice pair of moccasins or an African indigo blanket;
a lacy blouse or a stoneware birdhouse. It's hard to tell where one business
ends and the other begins, but I don't mind; it's all magic. The bright,
woodsy interior alone makes it worth a visit even if you aren't planning
on buying anything. But don't be surprised if you do as each object here
seems to be imbued with a fascinating back story.

CAZAMANCE CAFE

Outdoor Senegalese eatery

1102 East Cesar Chavez Street (78702) / +1 512 487 7222
cazamance.com / Closed Saturday-Monday

When Iba Thiam arrived in the U.S. from Senegal in 1996, he spoke not a word of English, but picked it up quickly working in the kitchens of New York. That's also where he honed his cooking skills; so well-honed that by 2010, he had opened his own place in Austin: Cazamance Cafe. Iba insists that passion is his food's first ingredient, and I'm inclined to agree with him: while the West African and Moroccan influences all but burst out of dishes like peanut butter stew and lamb meatballs, there's just a little something else I taste. Is it the cumin? The paprika? No – it's love.

P.S. On Sundays Cazamance is at HOPE Farmers' Market, on Comal Street.

CHARM SCHOOL VINTAGE

Dreamy vintage delights

2109 East Cesar Chavez Street (78702)   +1 512 344 9173
charmschoolvintage.com   Closed Monday

There's some kind of special pixie dust sprinkled on Charm School Vintage, a tiny shop you'll spend much more time in than you intend. Gorgeously stocked with pieces that range from antique, turn-of-the-century dresses to '90s grunge, the vibe here is more Stevie Nicks than Zooey Deschanel, with fringed gypsy coats, jewelry and beautiful leather bags eager for your next journey. Clothing here is pretty reasonable as far as quality vintage goes, and if you need outfit help, owner Shari Gerstenberger will pull together something spectacular.

COCO COQUETTE

A reason to join the Wig Party

2109 East Cesar Chavez Street (78702) / +1 512 344 9173
coco-coquette.com / Closed Monday

The absolute best place in town to play dress-up, Coco Coquette is glamazon headquarters for wig enthusiasts, fake lash addicts and lingerie connoisseurs. It's the kind of spot that'll make you want to invent an occasion to get yourself all dolled up in a blue Marie Antoinette mop or a cotton candy bob. Their menu of "wig parties" allows for fabulous groupings where everyone goes home with a wig and photographic documentation of their folly (each party comes with a photo booth).

EAST SIDE SHOW ROOM

1920's inspired restaurant and bar

1100 East 6th Street (78702) / +1 512 467 4280
eastsideshowroom.com / Open daily

When local designer and welder Mickie Danae Spencer – along with her sister and mother – opened East Side Show Room in 2010, it was bursting at the seams with a young and glittering clientele who often waited hours for a table. Nowadays, it's less frantic and more refined: the seasonal menu has matured into a confident French/New American fusion, drinks are creative and elegant, and service is snappy. The only thing that hasn't changed is the beautiful people: in keeping with ESSR's European, early 20th-century trappings, patrons here enjoy getting dressed up for each other.

HELM BOOTS

Crafted men's boots and accessories

900 East 6th Street (78702) / +1 512 609 8150 / helmboots.com
Closed Monday and Tuesday

Run like a boutique but arranged like a gallery, HELM Boots is enough to bring out the inner fashionista in the gruffest of men. Probably because the boots are handmade, each pair is priced to reflect the care that goes into shaping it. Indeed, HELM calls forth a time when clothes and accessories were an investment, and things were made to last. Alongside the boots, there are also big, bad Zippo lighters and handcrafted, leather man-purses. You get the feeling that within these walls, quality still trumps quantity, every time.

HILLSIDE FARMACY

Charming cure for hunger and sobriety

**1209 East 11th Street (78702) / +1 512 628 0168 / hillsidefarmacy.com
Open daily**

With a culinary compass turned squarely toward farms, Chef Sonya Cote's relationships with local produce providers are tight, and her food places a high premium on fresh, flavorful plants. At her casual yet elegant East Side bistro, those plants play just as large a role on the menu as proteins, turning simple dishes into subtle, satisfying executions. Sandwiches have fresh strawberry jam or fried green tomatoes slipped inside; dinners get a dose of jalapeño vinaigrette or celery root purée. It's these small touches that make the offerings so unique, and the space is downright adorable, too – like the name suggests, it's modeled after a vintage pharmacy.

JUSTINE'S BRASSERIE

Hearty French fare

4710 East 5th Street (78702) / +1 512 385 2900 / justines1937.com
Open daily

Way out on a dark road near nothing else much at all, Justine's Brasserie lies ready to seduce you with all its lusty charms. I say "seduce" because that is consistently the feeling I get here – that, no matter how long the table wait or how crowded the bar, I'm too taken with the early 20th-century style and the sultry waitresses to mind. Food-wise, it's French comfort through and through with trusty old standbys – think escargot in garlic and herb butter sauce, onion soup – none of which intend to blow your mind with creativity, but rather coat your tongue with sigh-inducing pleasure (and butter – lots of butter).

QUI

Playground of an Austin culinary star

1600 East 6th Street (78702) / **+1 512 436 9626** / **quiaustin.com**
Closed Sunday

The atmosphere at qui, the buzzy eatery from Austin's favorite culinary son
Paul Qui, is all hustle and flow. The cooks themselves serve you what they've
whipped up in the open kitchen because Paul wants to encourage his team's
imagination to roam free. There's an "idea wall" where the kitchen staff
scrawls down ingredient combinations they'd love to try, and unlike Paul's
Asian-rooted food trailer chain, East Side King, the menu here changes
every single day. This is not a place that hangs its hat on certain dishes.
Rather, qui is a place to come and enjoy the show, and to put your trust in
extraordinarily good hands.

SALT & TIME

A modern salumeria

**1912 East 7th Street (78702) / +1 512 524 1383 / saltandtime.com
Closed Monday**

Like the name implies, excellent meat only requires a couple of key
essentials. Besides seasoning and patience, Salt & Time is also a place
that prizes artisanal butchery skills, relationships with Texas ranches, and
impeccable curing. There's a full lunch and dinner menu here, not to
mention a small grocery, but the real reason to go is the salumi: rich, thin
slices of paprika-laced, oregano-flecked and pecan-studded varieties are
all for sale here, and they're all tasty.

SWOOP HOUSE

Charming supper club

3012 Gonzales Street (78762) / +1 512 467 6600 / supperfriends.com
By reservation only

Swoop House, headquarters of Swoop Events, is a restored 1930s bungalow transported from Hyde Park to the East Side, and is just impossibly pretty. The hard wood floors creak just right, a magenta chandelier sparkles overhead. Local farms supply the bulk of ingredients, which Chef Leanne Valenti fashions into plates such as beignet-like croutons atop peppery greens, garden-fresh gazpacho, or miniature pots of velvety chocolate mousse. What I love most about Swoop House is the intimacy, and the feeling that you're not dining at a restaurant, but in a room full of friends. Even if they are brand new ones.

TAKE HEART

Artisan gifts and cards

**1111 East 11th Street (78702) / +1 512 520 9664 / takeheartshop.com
Closed Monday**

Before being a curator was a fashionable career choice, I suspect Take Heart owner Nina Gordon was already a master of good taste. Her gift shop is a study in special, with small batches of soy candles clustered next to soft linen scarves, goats milk soaps piled in small stacks, clever cards marching along a wall. You get the impression that not only is everything here beautiful, but selected because it has a personal story behind it: a story that, like Nina's, arcs with artistic individuals trying to contribute something thoughtful to the world.

east austin art studios

Artistic delights

BIG MEDIUM
Building 2, 916 Springdale Road (78702) and 5305 Bolm Road
(78721), +1 512 939 6665, bigmedium.org, closed Sunday

BLUE GENIE ART INDUSTRIES
Building 4, 916 Springdale Road (78702), +1 512 444 6655
bluegenieart.com, open during November

EAST AUSTIN STUDIO TOUR
Various locations, +1 512 939 6665, eastaustinstudiotour.com
open during November

FISTERRA STUDIO
1200 East 2nd Street (78702), +1 512 482 0747, fisterrastudio.com
check the online calendar for opening

PUMP ART PROJECT
702 Shady Lane (78702), +1 512 351 8571, pumpproject.org
check the online calendar for opening

This swath of Austin is home to hundreds of artists, including wood workers, welders, painters, large scale fabricators. Take **Fisterra Studio** for example, the gallery and home of painter/sculptor Jennifer Chenoweth, who adorns her walls with works by other artist provocateurs. A few blocks further east you'll find **Pump Art Project**, a buzzing, two-story hive of multimedia workers, and down the road, the gallery and artist space **Big Medium**. Its individual rooms are chock full of painters, photographers and jewelry designers, not to mention the lively folks behind **Blue Genie Art Industries**, a specialty shop for enormous structures and whacky Austin business signage.

If you happen to be in Austin during November, then lucky, lucky you, for you'll get to attend **East Austin Studio Tour**, a magical walking or biking tour of these studios and others. Unlike a regular gallery opening, artists open their studios for public viewing during EAST, many of them serving soup and hot chocolate right out of their own kitchens.

FISTERRA STUDIO

south congress

travis heights

Just across the river from downtown Austin lies South Congress, a 24/7 carnival of Keep Austin Weird culture. Now granted, that "weirdness" currently has a shiny, touristy scaffolding, but it's still one of the first places Austinites bring their relatives to visit. That's because it's a joy to walk up and down admiring South Congress's flashing lights, adorable cafés, vintage stores and historical institutions such as The Continental Club (see pg 126), a burlesque club turned music venue. You'll also find food trailers aplenty here, each peddling delicious eats with high-quality ingredients, so go ahead – grab a snack. You'll need it to traverse this long, lovely hub of Austin creativity.

1 Allen's Boots
2 Big Top Candy Shop
3 Blackmail Boutique
4 Home Slice Pizza
5 Snack Bar
6 South Congress Cafe
7 Stag
8 Yard Dog Art Gallery

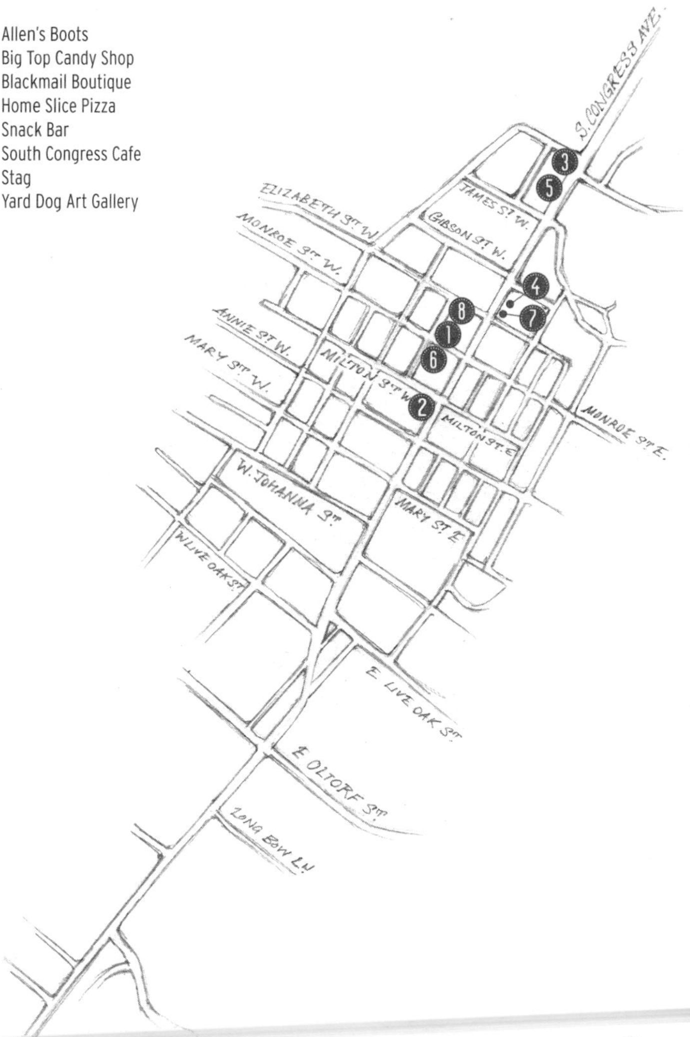

ALLEN'S BOOTS

Sprawling boot city

1522 South Congress Avenue (78704) / +1 512 447 1413
allensboots.com / Open daily

Did you know that it is illegal to visit, or reside in, the city of Austin without owning a pair of cowboy boots? If not an actual law, it's a law of Texas manners anyway. So if you don't own a pair, correct this infraction with a trip to Allen's Boots, where the walls smell of leather and shelves go on for city blocks. Here, you'll find understated Frye's, tooled leather lace-ups, and rhinestone-covered knee-highs with enough bling to blind you. Prices range from about $70 to $3000, so be prepared to drop a chunk of change — but then these boots weren't just made for walkin'. They're eye-poppin', too.

BIG TOP CANDY SHOP

Confectionery sold, circus conjured

1706 South Congress Avenue (78704) / +1 512 462 2220
bigtopcandyshop.tumblr.com / Open daily

Like the circus itself, Big Top Candy Shop skates that fine line between sweet and creepy; nostalgic and freaky. Packed with almost every sweet known to mankind, including about 80 different varieties of taffy and something called "Public Enemy's MICHECK DA CANDY", it's decked out with old circus posters, rusted musical instruments and carnival minutiae perfect for a novelty store or, conversely, a circus-themed haunted house. It's ideal for those looking for weirdo stuff to take home.

BLACKMAIL BOUTIQUE

High-end goth

1202 South Congress Avenue (78704) / +1 512 804 5881
blackmailboutique.com / Open daily

Housed in what was once an 1889 mercantile shop and operated by a fashion designer, Blackmail Boutique is a bewitching little spot for fashion and gifts that lean darker, edgier, punkier. Drapey and couture, many of the clothes on display here are made by Gail Chovan, the store's heart, soul and owner. Here you'll find upscale clothing brands and interesting, artistic items for the home such as black-and-white photo prints, unique sculpture and ornate plates not meant to be eaten on, but mounted on the wall and

HOME SLICE PIZZA

Pie you'll scoff in a New York minute

1415 South Congress Avenue (78704) / +1 512 444 7437
homeslicepizza.com / Open daily

When Home Slice Pizza entered the scene in 2006, locals descended on it en masse, necessitating a second, overflow takeout shop – "More Home Slice" – right next door. Specializing in New York-style pizza, slices here are thick and generous, with their crust crisped to just-right thinness. Whole pies offer lots of topping variety (clams, anyone?), but if you happen to get there while they're serving The Sicilian – it's somewhat seasonal – order it. Unlike Home Slice's signature crust, this dough is airy, chewier and, like traditional Sicilian pizza, the cheese is underneath the sauce, making each bite knee-bucklingly juicy.

SNACK BAR

Local eats, global perspective

1224 South Congress Avenue (78704) / +1 512 445 2626
snackbaraustin.com / Open daily

 "Why, sometimes I've believed as many as six impossible things before breakfast," said the White Queen to Alice in *Through the Looking Glass*. Gazing at Snack Bar's brunch menu you may feel similarly, given how it combines local, seasonal fare with a penchant for global cuisine. It's on and off the menu, but the Tamago Yoko is one of my go-to brunches, combining as it does three of my favorite things: bacon, sriracha and wasabi (yep – it's hot). But whether we're talking brunch or dinner, Snack Bar has this special knack for glamorizing vegetables – see the simple-sounding "Farm Salad", topped with creamy, from-scratch ricotta. So eat up your greens here!

SOUTH CONGRESS CAFE

New America meets Latin America

1600 South Congress Avenue (78704) / +1 512 447 3905
southcongresscafe.com / Open daily

South Congress Cafe has long been a south Austin institution, a modish eatery known for crab cakes and creative mimosas. Since Chef Cesar Ortiz took the helm the food has taken a nice step forward. Incorporating Cajun and Latin flavors into the menu's New American staples, there are several standouts here – such as the buttery pan-roasted scallops in cauliflower cream, and the duck and oyster gumbo spiced with juicy jalapeño sausage. My favorite on the brunch list, though, is Ortiz's take on chilaquiles, which is much more vegetable-y than the traditional variety: he mixes in crunchy kale, beet and sweet potato chips.

STAG

The Man's man store

1423 South Congress Avenue (78704) / +1 512 373 7824
stagaustin.com / Open daily

To reach back into the '90s lexicon vault, the vibe at Stag is far from
metrosexual. Oh no. As the name might suggest, it's all man. The type of
man who eschews designer stubble in favor of a full beard that he trims
only with polished tools; the type who reads Hemingway, possibly dons
a pocket square, and lives by the mantra that clothes maketh the man.
If you or your red-blooded male friend fancies leather footwear, checked
shirts and masculine accessories, look no further than Stag.

YARD DOG ART GALLERY

Novel art and crafts gallery

1510 South Congress Avenue (78704) / +1 512 912 1613 / yarddog.com
Open daily

There's an unfinished, rough-around-the-edges feel to Yard Dog, and the work on display is more haunting than haute. Originally opened in the mid '90s as a Southern folk art gallery, it is now somewhat genre-less, and yet there's definitely a conversation happening between pieces here. Paint, ink or mixed medium, artists espouse an almost punk rock attitude toward the enterprise of art itself, which isn't to say the work isn't serious. On the contrary: Yard Dog's owners are attracted to wry outsider art, pop art and fantastical pieces that place a high premium on craft, be it in the form of a Sean Connery wood carving or paper cut monsters.

JO CLAUWAERT
Skeleton Mask
$600

JO CLAUWAERT
Hendrix Mask
$600

vintage shopping

Go-to shops for throwback threads

AMELIA'S RETRO VOGUE AND RELICS
2213 South 1st Street (78704), +1 512 442 4446
ameliasretrovogue.com, closed Sunday and Monday

BLUE VELVET VINTAGE CLOTHING
217 West North Loop (78751), +1 512 452 2583, bluevelvetaustin.com
open daily

FEATHERS BOUTIQUE
1700 South Congress Avenue (78704), +1 512 912 9779
feathersboutiquevintage.com, open daily

NEW BOHEMIA
1606 South Congress Avenue (78704), +1 512 326 1238
tumblr.com/blog/newbohemiaatx, open daily

PROTOTYPE VINTAGE DESIGN
1700 1/2 South Congress Avenue (78704), +1 512 447 7686
prototypevintagedesign.net, open daily

ROOM SERVICE VINTAGE
107 East North Loop Boulevard (78751), +1 512 451 1057
roomservicevintage.com, open daily

UNCOMMON OBJECTS
1512 South Congress Avenue (78704), +1 512 442 4000
uncommonobjects.com, open daily

VACANCY ROAD
2810 Manchaca Road (78704), +1 512 462 4510
vacancyroad.tumblr.com, open daily

While it's still socially acceptable in most parts of the city to saunter around in your flip flops and lake-ready cutoffs, that doesn't mean Austinites don't enjoy getting a little dolled up every now and then. Our preferred style poison? Vintage. Not only because it looks rad, but also because we can afford it. You'll find no greater concentration of pre-loved than on South Congress, where **New Bohemia** and **Uncommon Objects** beckon you in off the street. In New Bohemia you can dress up yourself; in Uncommon Objects, you'll find things to dress up your house: it's stuffed with funky, hip finds, ranging from mounted fiddles to dainty lace fans.

Around the corner on Milton Street, two impossibly cool boutiques neighbor each other: **Prototype Vintage Design** and **Feathers Boutique**. Both feature excellent, well-curated collections but if a line had to be drawn, it would be that Prototype offers more leather and knits, Feathers more sparkles and spikes.

Down south you'll find two additional vintage destinations: **Amelia's Retro Vogue and Relics** and **Vacancy Road**. Amelia's is a way, way back machine of mid-1800s to mid-1900s finds; anyone with an affinity for Edwardian, Victorian or hats will do well here. Vacancy Road, on the other hand, is a treasure-trove of throwback furniture and homewares, mostly from the 1950s-70s.

Finally, North Loop (technically 53rd Street), a strip of colorful Austin oddities all by itself, has two shops I just adore – **Blue Velvet Vintage** and **Room Service Vintage**. I've found several easy cotton dresses at Blue Velvet, whose petite interior manages to pack in a surprising amount of variety. Meanwhile Room Service has helped me decorate just about every Austin home I've lived in, with their ever-rotating stock of killer furniture and lighting. Just be quick: items are priced to sell, and sell they do in a flash.

———◆———

south austin

south lamar, south first, oak hill

A large area primarily covering the coveted 78704 zip code, South Austin is another word for "hip". Here, swanky new restaurants mix with understated, neighborhood coffee shops; boutiques glimmer with a studied cool and there's a gorgeous-yet-funky home on every corner. For music lovers, it's here that ACL Music Festival touches down annually (in Zilker Park), and it's the neighborhood where "cosmic cowboys" such as Willie Nelson found their following (specifically, at the Broken Spoke and much-mourned Armadillo World Headquarters). With more food trailers than you can shake a stick at, it's also a place where foodies can indulge to their heart's content.

1 Craft
2 Elizabeth Street Café
3 Henri's
4 Lenoir
5 Lick
6 MOSS Designer Consignment
7 South Austin Gallery
8 The Herb Bar
9 The Natural Gardener (off map)
10 The Stitch Lab
11 Uchi
12 Whip In (off map)
13 W3ll People

CRAFT

Playful handiwork house

**1632 South 1st Street (78704) / +1 512 900 9957 / craft-austin.com
Closed Monday**

For the times when you're suddenly overcome by the urge to cover your
room in God's eyes or knit scarves for everybody you know, Craft is the
material-filled, pay-by-the-hour place to do it. Organized by hobby and
stocked with rad inventory, it's $10 per hour (plus supplies) to make
anything you want — and a measly $5 per hour if you bring your own
supplies. They also hold 25 per cent off "Crafty Hours" where you can
learn to make seasonal goodies, like Christmas tree ornaments or
Dia de los Muertos "sugar skulls".

ELIZABETH STREET CAFÉ

Hip French-Vietnamese

1501 South 1st Street (78704) / +1 512 291 2881
elizabethstreetcafe.com / Open daily

Judging by the breathless "OMG"s that accompany customer photos of Elizabeth Street Café's dishes on Twitter, one gets the idea that food here reduces you to few words and fewer descriptors. I think that's because patrons are so taken with the 360-degree delectable experience that the café creates, from the light-filled ambience to Vietnamese dishes such as grilled octopus salad – the patiently braised tentacles are little bites of joy with the lemony kohlrabi they rest on. In cooler weather, order a steaming bowl of pho. The pork broth option is more decadent than your traditional version, especially when you order it with morsels of Niman Ranch pork belly.

HENRI'S

Sexy wine and cheese lounge

2026 South Lamar Boulevard (78704) / +1 512 442 3373
henrischeese.com / Open daily

Cheese is that most democratic of foods, able to transform itself both into demure pairing plates and gooey grilled snacks best approached with heedless gluttony. You can do both at Henri's, which operates as a café by day, and a seductive, low-lit lounge by night. Bottles of wine line the entry wall and cheese selections glow from the front counter's display case; further back, tables cluster in cozy, tavern-like corners. I like to order a cheese plate with friends, asking our server for a variety that ranges from the mild and tame to the bordering-on-gym-socks-scented. We always lick the plate clean.

LENOIR

Romantic prix fixe

1807 South 1st Street (78704) / +1 512 215 9778
lenoirrestaurant.com / Closed Monday

It's hard to talk about Lenoir without descending into a cascade of sighs
– that's the effect it has on you. Selected the year of its opening as one of
Bon Appétit magazine's "Top 50 New Restaurants", Lenoir is a converted
cottage that seats 34 people max. That's a good thing actually, all the
better to savor a meal sans hustle and bustle, a meal lovingly concocted by
husband and wife team Todd Duplechan and Jessica Maher. A little French,
a little Asian, a little Cajun; here's a taste of the seasonal prix fixe menu:
lime brown butter on char pasta, coconut polenta, imperial stout chocolate
cake. These are bites to linger over.

LICK

Artisanal ice cream

2032 South Lamar Boulevard (78704) / +1 512 363 5622
ilikelick.com / Open daily

While big cities like Chicago and San Francisco usually lead the way in trendy eating, it's a small town mentality that inspired Lick. Co-owners Chad and Anthony grew up eating ice cream from local mom 'n' pops, where fruit was farm-fresh and the milk practically walked itself over. Inspired by their childhoods and Austin's abundant locavore scene, they launched Lick with a simple mission in mind: to create unique flavors with the highest quality ingredients possible. The result? Wildly creative flavors such as goat cheese, fig and honey; candied tomato, basil and balsamic; and cardamom pear cake — all without a drop of high fructose corn syrup in sight.

MOSS DESIGNER CONSIGNMENT

Designer resale clothing

705B South Lamar Boulevard (78704) / +1 512 916 9961
mossaustin.com / Open daily

Every time I walk into MOSS Designer Consignment, I feel like my taste is improving just by being in such close proximity to nice things. It focuses on designer labels, with each piece being lovingly selected and essentially brand new: Jimmy Choos sparkle from display shelves, evening gowns from Gaultier beckon me to an imaginary red carpet. Started by two fashionable women who already had retail success with Feathers (see pg 72), MOSS's wares are just as luxe as you'd find at a traditional boutique, but cost about 25–30 per cent less. If, like me, you need help gettin' dressed fancy, the ladies also have a blog with fun styling tips.

SOUTH AUSTIN GALLERY

Artistic gifts, vinyl and tailored vintage clothing

507A West Mary Street (78704) / +1 512 680 4018
southaustingallery.com / Open daily

Packed into a petite space, you'll find well-curated vinyl, original photography prints and Austin-themed décor in South Austin Gallery. There's also another reason to adore this shop: while it isn't a vintage store proper, it always has a few tidy racks of sweet throwbacks that have been tailored into modern shapes and styles. Case in point: until karma and a sewing machine intervened, my striped summer romper enjoyed a previous life as a high-necked muumuu. I bought it along with one of my favorite pieces of art — a photograph of a ramshackle island hut, shot by one of the store's owners — and an old Marvin Gaye record in perfect condition. This place may be small, but it's a treasure trove of goodies.

THE HERB BAR

A good witch's den of herbs and cures

200 West Mary Street (78704) / +1 512 444 6251 / theherbbar.com
Closed Sunday

I often joke that I could happily move into The Herb Bar, but I'm only halfway kidding about that. A tiny, foliage-covered cottage that opens up into a den of tinctures, goat milk soaps, and tarot cards, it's both a gift shop and a genuine herbal pharmacy. Here, you can tell employees precisely what ails you and off they go to find your personalized, holistic remedy – though you could also spend the better part of an hour just browsing. It's a great lair of cures and curiosities, one I like to pop into whenever I'm in the area.

THE NATURAL GARDENER

A utopia for the horticultural

8648 Old Bee Caves Road (78735) / +1 512 288 6113
naturalgardeneraustin.com / Open daily

It's quite a drive to get to The Natural Gardener, but it's worth the gas.
When I first found it, I thought I had stumbled into my idea of heaven:
flowers as far as the eye could see; colorful barns; a soundtrack of wind
chimes. The grounds are so vast that I was a little nervous, walking
around with my crumpled list of plants and attempting to navigate the
abundance, but I need not have worried. Soon enough, a wild-haired
woman grabbed a wheelbarrow and helped me find everything I needed,
helping me to rehab both my yard and my sense of plant competence.

THE STITCH LAB

Craft classes for the modern Martha

1000 South 1st Street (78704) / +1 512 440 0712 / stitchlab.biz
Open daily

Every time you swipe your card for something rectangular-shaped – say, a pillowcase – doesn't a tiny part of you think, "SERIOUSLY? I could make this!"? Well, it's time to put your money where your mouth is. The fine teachers at Stitch Lab can teach you how to sew all sorts of things, from the elementary (a canvas bag) to the advanced (bathing suits), with tons of fun in between. There's instruction for dressmaking, knitting/crocheting, even DIY fashion design, as well as a shop for all your fabric, thread, ribbons and trimmings needs.

UCHI

Austin's grand dame of sushi

801 South Lamar Boulevard (78704) / +1 512 916 4808
uchiaustin.com / Open daily

For talented young chefs, Uchi's kitchen (and that of sister restaurant Uchiko in North Austin) is somewhat like Harvard: only the best and the brightest get in. Chef Tyson Cole has cultivated an exacting yet experimental program at his original crown jewel restaurant, and as a result, Uchi has become a culinary pilgrimage for gourmands everywhere. Expect sushi and other Japanese dishes that deliver layers of taste, like arrowhead squid tentacles cooked sous-vide for five hours then charred and laid atop a creamy, puréed parsley root. The desserts are no less inventive: one involves mesquite pods, which to you and me look like bumpy sticks that fall out of trees in central Texas. To Uchi, they look like a potential panna cotta, paired with huckleberry and gingerbread sand.

WHIP IN

Live music, booze and Indian food

1950 IH 35 (78704) / +1 512 442 5337 / whipin.com / Open daily

There's a lot going on at Whip In. Once a gas station-cum-beer-and-wine-store, it's now a brewery, a "dhabapub", a food market and live music venue (but not a gas station). Replete with kitschy Indian-themed art and loads of craft brews, the interior is so delightful you might miss the patio out back – but don't! The picnic tables are surrounded by kale, the music is fantastic and the crowd is a mix of mustachioed hipsters and Austin old-timers absorbing a feast of riches. Speaking of which: hunker down with a hot panaani (panini served on naan bread) and a *kombucha* (a fermented tea drink) on tap for a simple, appetizing meal.

W3LL PEOPLE

Posh makeup, natural ingredients

215 South Lamar Boulevard / +1 512 366 7963 / w3llpeople.com
Open daily

While elsewhere in Texas you may find a "the higher the hair, the closer to God" beauty ethic, here in Austin, it's all about stripped-down and natural. A sophisticated beauty shop with a generous dose of hippie wisdom, W3ll People peddles all-natural makeup that eschews toxins for green tea, and artificial fragrances for omega 3's. Abiding by the philosophy that our skin absorbs 60–80 per cent of what we put on it, W3ll People makes their own stuff using ingredients we should probably all be getting a bit more of anyway: lavender, essential fatty acids, aloe, plus a slew of other organic and food-grade items.

indie bookstores

Havens of the printed page

In a high-tech city besot by Kindles and iPads, there's nothing I enjoy more than stepping into a real bookstore: the pretty covers, the handwritten employee suggestions, that distinctly musty smell. Award-winning **BookPeople** is Austin's ground zero for quality reading (adult and children's titles), as well as quirky toys and cards – not to mention weekly tour stops by famous authors.

Farewell Books, the descendent of dearly departed Domy Books, is equal parts avante garde literature and art gallery – the place you come for obscure Proust, and walk out with an original sketch of a robot unicorn.

Malvern Books champions lesser-known publishers and poetry presses, and is the ideal spot to curl up with a brand new discovery. And finally, **BookWoman**, Austin's feminist bookstore, not only stocks socially conscious reads but holds open mic poetry nights where you can share your herstory.

BOOKPEOPLE
603 North Lamar Boulevard (78703), +1 512 472 5050
bookpeople.com, open daily

BOOKWOMAN
5501 North Lamar Boulevard (78751), +1 512 472 2785
ebookwoman.com, open daily

FAREWELL BOOKS
913 East Cesar Chavez Street (78702), +1 512 473 2665
farewellbookstore.com, open daily

MALVERN BOOKS
613, West 29th Street (78705), +1 512 322 2097, malvernbooks.com
closed Monday

clarksville and tarrytown

mount bonnell

With loads of coffee shops and wine bars squeezed into tiny bungalows, plus one of the prettiest museums in town – all scattered among some of the city's most jaw-dropping homes – you could cook up quite a pleasant day for yourself in this hilly corner of Austin. The nice thing about Clarksville and Tarrytown is that they offer a choose-your-own-adventure of fanciness, affording you both upscale dining and shopping (caviar at Jeffrey's, see pg 94; cashmere at By George, see pg 92), as well as laid-back socializing (ideally over an old-school ice cream float at Nau's Enfield Drug, see pg 96). If you're here during the holidays, this is also a great place to tool around in a car and gawk at Christmas lights: no other neighborhood does them as lavishly.

1 By George
2 Clark's Oyster Bar
3 Jeffrey's
4 Mozart's Coffee Roasters
5 Nau's Enfield Drug
6 Sabia
7 The Contemporary Austin (Laguna Gloria)
8 The Winflo Osteria

BY GEORGE

Upscale fashion in an unpretentious atmosphere

524 North Lamar Boulevard (78703) / +1 512 472 5951
bygeorgeaustin.com / Open daily

Like the proverbial angel and devil on your shoulder, By George's virtues are abundant, but it's dangerous how much you'll covet. Named one of the Top Ten Boutiques in the U.S. by *Lucky Magazine*, this has long been the spot in Austin where natty gents and ladies come to for high-end labels like YSL, Derek Lam, Rag & Bone. The knowledgeable staff can help you find just the right fit, recommending brands that suit both your body-type and taste, so you'll walk out looking — and feeling — like a million dollars.

CLARK'S OYSTER BAR

Tasty seafood, sailing club comfort

1200 West 6th Street (78703) / +1 512 297 2525 / clarksoysterbar.com
Open daily

Nautical and preppy, there's nowhere else like Clark's Oyster Bar in Austin.
Probably because it feels like a mini Cape Cod, what with the striped
awnings, white-washed walls and overall feeling of espadrilles. With
oysters flown in daily from both coasts (British Columbia and Nova Scotia),
the regional menu is long and deliciously diverse; ask a server to help you
pick out your favorite flavor. There's also first-class caviar from places as
far-flung as Israel and China, but even humbler meals, such as the generous
crab cake and pan roasted hamburger (topped with melted gruyère), are
handled with beautiful care. Next time I'm on my yacht, I'll ask Clark's
to cater.

JEFFREY'S

Elder statesman of steakhouses

1204 West Lynn Street (78703) / +1 512 477 5584 / jeffreysofaustin.com
Open daily

At its core, Jeffrey's is a fine-dining steakhouse, with a long legacy of congressmen and other distinguished regulars as customers. In recent years, it's undergone a renovation and menu overhaul that has made the always-elegant menu more contemporary, drawing in all kinds of diners with a heightened sense of flavor possibility. Steaks are still king, but dishes like the persimmon and duck confit salad give you an idea of where things are headed now; brown butter crème fraîche makes this appetizer even more interesting and luxurious. Despite the changes, this is still a place where old-fashioned restaurant values matter: the service is polished, the acoustics are good, and there's even a roaring fire. Classics get their status for a reason.

MOZART'S COFFEE ROASTERS

Pastries and java with a lake view

3825 Lake Austin Boulevard (78703) / +1 512 477 2900
mozartscoffee.com / Open daily

So, here's what you do with Mozart's. Pick a sunny, obscenely beautiful day in Austin, wake up early and dress for outdoor seating. Next, select a table on the wide wooden deck that affords you a sparkling view of Lake Austin, and send your companion for coffee and a slice of tres leches cake. Ignore that reasonable voice that objects to cake for breakfast. Bask in the utterly charming atmosphere of low-hanging trees and craggy stone walls that Mozart's has cultivated, eat your breakfast one delighted bite at a time, and marvel at the good fortune of life itself. Tomorrow morning, if time and space allows, repeat.

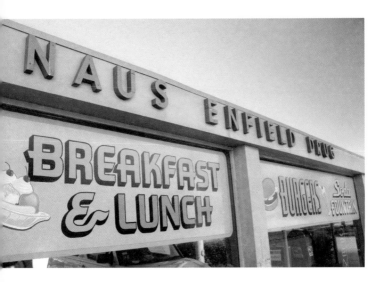

NAU'S ENFIELD DRUG

Austin's last soda fountain

1115 West Lynn Street (78703) / +1 512 476 1221 / nausdrug.com.
Open daily

Technically, Nau's is a neighborhood drugstore, but in Austin it's also the last of a gently dying breed: the 1950s soda fountain. Generations of folks have come here for years to slurp down thick milkshakes and ice cream floats, seated around the curvy counter or squeezed into wooden booths. Back to the milkshakes: on a blistering summer day, there's no greater indulgence than a chocolate malted shake, best enjoyed with a melty, grilled cheese sandwich. Maybe it's the dairy, but more likely the nostalgia, that makes both taste so satisfying.

SABIA

Holistic beauty

**1213 West 5th Street (78703) / +1 512 469 0447 / sabia.com
Open daily**

"I have the simplest tastes", Oscar Wilde once said. "I am always satisfied with the best." Such could be said of Sabia, a sleek downtown apothecary for organic gorgeousity. In addition to their vast selection of beauty goods from the likes of Kiehl's, Dr. Hauschka and Aesop, they also offer in-house haircuts and color, as well as all-natural facials that leave skin supermodel dewy. Speaking of skin, look out for an Austin-based line here called Inventive Eco-Organics: in addition to being local, the prices are shockingly reasonable given the quality of ingredients.

THE CONTEMPORARY AUSTIN (LAGUNA GLORIA)

Waterfront villa turned art museum

3809 West 35th Street (78703) / +1 512 458 8191
thecontemporaryaustin.org / Closed Monday

A wide-lawned, 1916 Italianate-style villa that looks over Lake Austin, this is just about the most glamorous spot in town. It's also an art museum, but ever since its mission turned in the direction of contemporary art, there's a new dynamic. Art classes for children and families are held here too, and if you're in Austin early fall, you might catch one of the most extravagant foodie events of the year: the annual La Dolce Vita Food & Wine Festival, which brings together more than 50 Austin restaurants and wineries for a classy (if slightly bacchanalian) night of tastings.

THE WINFLO OSTERIA

Classic Italian, modern trappings

1315 West 6th Street (78703) / +1 512 582 1027 / winfloosteria.com
Open daily

Shaded by a large oak tree on a quieter stretch of 6th Street, The Winflo Osteria manages to be two things at once: an old school Italian eatery and a super hip hangout. Opened by two siblings and Italophiles, Winflo relishes in rich Italian classics such as lasagne bolognese and quattro formaggi pizza, but also allows Austin's local leanings to push the menu creatively. For instance, their chipotle cannelloni almost look like Italian enchiladas and taste just as decadent, courtesy of the spicy chipotle cream sauce within. Tip: there's also a basement "listening room" downstairs, so check the schedule to catch an intimate acoustic show after dinner.

outdoor oases

Austin's natural beauty

AUDITORIUM SHORES
800 West Riverside Drive (78704), +1 512 974 6700
facebook.com/auditoriumshores

BARTON SPRINGS POOL
2201 Barton Springs Road (78704), +1 512 476 9044
austintexas.gov/department/barton-springs-pool

BULL CREEK
6701 Lakewood Drive (78731), +1 512 477 1566, bullcreek.net

DEEP EDDY POOL
401 Deep Eddy Avenue (78703), +1 512 472 8546
austintexas.gov/department/deep-eddy-pool

HAMILTON POOL
24300 Hamilton Pool Road, Dripping Springs (78620), +1 512 264 2740
co.travis.tx.us/tnr/parks/hamilton_pool.asp

KRAUSE SPRINGS
404 Krause Spring Road, Spicewood (78669), +1 830 693 4181
krausesprings.net

MOUNT BONNELL
3800 Mount Bonnell Road (78731), +1 512 477 1566
austinparks.org/our-parks.html?parkid=287

While concrete jungles like New York induce pulse-racing excitement, the thing I've always adored about Austin is its easy green. There are parks and waterways everywhere, including the city's crown jewel, **Barton Springs Pool**: a South Austin mecca for families, hippies and everyone in between. Come here or **Deep Eddy Pool** for a lazy day in the sun, both of which afford you swimming and sunbathing right in the middle of town.

Auditorium Shores provides a gorgeous backdrop for a mid-day walk, while **Bull Creek** – sunken in a verdant North Austin valley – is like a secret park for hiking and creek wallowing.

Mount Bonnell isn't far away, and as the highest point in Austin, it's one of the most popular places in town for wedding proposals.

Just out of Austin city limits, **Krause Springs** beckons with a huge expanse of water, while mystical **Hamilton Pool**, with its deep translucence and giant rock overhangs, is an oasis that calls for all-day relaxation.

MOUNT BONNELL

allandale and rosedale

brentwood

Once upon a time, Burnet Road was "Burnet Freeway", a long, straight stretch of concrete that led you from Travis County right out of Austin city limits. Burnet Road, which cuts through the middle of Allandale and Rosedale, still bears traces of that freeway-past with funky old diners and roadside antique shops galore. Yet what was once the very outskirts of town has now been swallowed whole by local business. This is a place where old Austin happily mingles with the new. A place where you can bite into juicy burgers from a '70s drive-in or nibble on an artisanal cheese plate from an airy French café. Like my dad, who loves showing off his newly acquired hipster vocabulary ("OMG, Tolly"), this is an area of town whose non-hipster roots show through quite endearingly.

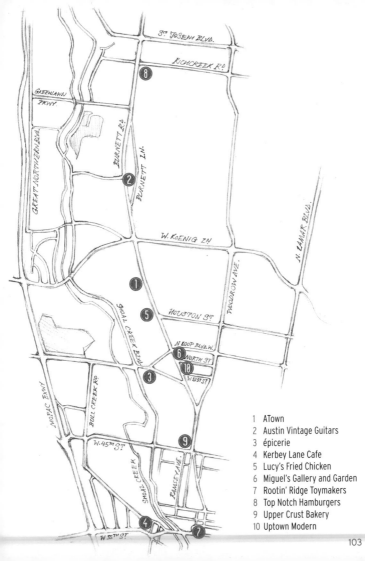

1 ATown
2 Austin Vintage Guitars
3 épicerie
4 Kerbey Lane Cafe
5 Lucy's Fried Chicken
6 Miguel's Gallery and Garden
7 Rootin' Ridge Toymakers
8 Top Notch Hamburgers
9 Upper Crust Bakery
10 Uptown Modern

ATOWN

Etsy-esque gifts and clothing

5502 Burnet Road (78756) | **+1 512 323 2533** | **shopatown.tumblr.com**
Open daily

ATown is filled wall-to-wall with artsy, handmade jewelry and clothing, screen-printed cards, and lovingly stitched stuffed animals. Almost everything here comes from local artists, several of whom I see popping in to replenish their wares, with backpacks full of wooden baubles or just-mixed soaps. It's now become my go-to stop for birthdays, the place where I can always find a unique little something for a friend — and admittedly

AUSTIN VINTAGE GUITARS

Instruments and gear, aged to perfection

6555 Burnet Road (78757) / +1 512 428 9100 / austinvintageguitars.com
Closed Sunday

Many a musician has made the sojourn to Austin to realize their on-stage dreams. And most probably wouldn't disagree if you accused them of a little geekmanship: the way their faces light up at the sight of a vintage Telecaster, the drooling over an amp from the time of the Carter administration. If you or your friends are like this, then a trip to Austin Vintage Guitars – which peddles much more than just guitars – will tickle you or them pink. The newer (larger) location makes room for even more inventory than their original South Austin home, and there's a repair shop in the back for when their beloved old stuff meets the limits of age.

ÉPICERIE

French-Louisiana cuisine in 1930s bungalow

2307 Hancock Drive (78756) / +1 512 371 6840 / epicerieaustin.com
Open daily

Remember Britney Spears singing "hit me baby, one more time"? That pretty much sums up my relationship with French-Louisiana eatery, épicerie, a place I visited three times in one week just after it opened – twice in a single day. Part café and part petite grocer, I couldn't resist dabbling in its cheese counter, its pastries and its menu proper during my first stop (lunch), and convinced an entirely new set of dining companions to go back with me later (dinner), so I could try the oxtail stew, the fried pickles – and more delicious cheese. As Britney would say, "Oops! I did it again."

KERBEY LANE CAFE

King of Austin diner-cafés

3704 Kerbey Lane (78731) / +1 512 451 1436 / kerbeylanecafe.com
Open daily (24hrs Thursday–Sunday)

Opened in 1980 on a wave of '70s post-hippie ethos and a burgeoning locavore movement, Kerbey Lane Cafe (the original) is a testament to Old Austin and the edibles that give our city character. High on this list are Kerbey queso (our version of holy ambrosia), breakfast tacos and bison Frito pie, a delicious mound of ground meat, black beans and corn chips, dripping with sour cream and grated cheddar. It's diner food alright, but with a heavy dose of both Texan and Austin culinary philosophies: a place where earthy, crunchy vegans can and do mix happily with hungry carnivores.

LUCY'S FRIED CHICKEN

Finger lickin' tasty

**5408 Burnet Road (78756) / +1 512 514 0664 / lucysfriedchicken.com
Open daily**

The second branch of Lucy's Fried Chicken in the city, I'm recommending this location to you because it was built inside the former home of another local institution: Austin Diner. Once that one moved up the road, Lucy's swept in on a river of buttermilk, and the marriage is beautiful: fried chicken has breathed new life into these hallowed walls, now encasing a hardworking kitchen with more than just deep fryers. Brining each piece of chicken in buttermilk for 24 hours ensures that each bite is a juicy one, and riffs on their signature (fried chicken nachos, fried chicken spaghetti) yield forkfuls of delicious sin.

MIGUEL'S GALLERY AND GARDEN

Mexican and Asian ceramics, pots and statues

5209 Burnet Road (78756) / +1 512 323 5563 / miguelsimports.com
Open daily (closed Monday in winter)

It's hard to miss the grand gates of Miguel's Gallery and Garden, which are flanked by a humble garage and a taco shop. Do turn into the little parking lot out front, though, because inside those gates is a vast expanse of artisan work: talavera ceramics from Mexico in every hue, carved stone planters from Bali, Buddha statues from the world over. Every corner of the property is chock-a-bloc with a new hand-carved this, a different metal-worked that. And while the sheer amount of stock is staggering, somehow this place manages to be so thoughtfully put together, so obviously well cared-for, that you can't help but linger.

ROOTIN' RIDGE TOYMAKERS

Handcrafted wooden playthings

1206 West 38th Street (78705) / +1 512 453 2604 / rootinridge.com
Closed Sunday and Monday (open daily in December)

In 1975 Paul Kyle found himself nearly out of work due to a recession that slammed his carpentry trade. But he still had leftover scraps, so he and his wife Georgean used them to make wooden toys for their friends and family for Christmas. Almost 40 years later, Paul and Georgean are still making them, and they are every bit as sweet and simple as ever. At their toyshop in central Austin, you won't find any flashing lights or battery-powered noises. You will find charmingly handcrafted animals, trains, games, puzzles and kaleidoscopes, as well as a windowed workshop where children can watch toys being made.

TOP NOTCH HAMBURGERS

Classic diner

7525 Burnet Road (78757) / +1 512 452 2181 / topnotchaustin.com
Open daily

A vintage drive-in from the early '70s, Top Notch Hamburgers was immortalized in the '90s, when director Richard Linklater put it in his film *Dazed and Confused*, which arguably launched Matthew McConaughey's acting career – Top Notch the scene of his trademark drawl "I git older, they stay the same age". These days the diner is still a film lovers' destination, with regular movie nights in the parking lot. Accompanied by delightfully greasy charcoal-broiled burgers and honey blonde onion rings (no Paleo menu here, folks), it's a date-night that works in any decade.

UPPER CRUST BAKERY

Hot, baked goodness

**4508 Burnet Road (78756) / +1 512 467 0102 / uppercrustbakery.com
Open daily**

There's magic lurking inside Upper Crust Bakery, in the form of dense cinnamon rolls, perfectly chewy gingerbread men, and rich brownies topped with toasted pecans. Everything is made from scratch at this almost 30-year-old European style bakery, which is family-run to boot, and maybe that's their secret. Before you sink your teeth into a single scone, you already feel cared for, already sense the warmth behind those glass displays. That and the childhood-evocative chocolate-laced air that swirls around every packed table.

UPTOWN MODERN

Mid-century heaven

5111 Burnet Road (78756) / +1 512 452 1200 / uptownmodernaustin.com
Open daily

Were this the 1960s, Uptown Modern is the place where Don and Megan Draper would shop to furnish their swanky Manhattan pad. It's not of course, but guess what? We're all obsessed with mid-century modern again. Fortunately, this 6,000-square-foot furniture shop can satisfy all your *Mad Men* design cravings, with sleek couches in kicky colors, mod coffee tables and sunburst mirrors galore. Also, one of the best vintage jewelry collections in town is sitting primly on the front register, in case you want to bring home something smaller than, say, a sofa.

north austin

north shoal creek, north burnet

The last bastion of Austin urban sprawl, North Austin is a funny animal. Sure, there are chains here – but there's also a goldmine of family-owned Asian joints, as well as an increasing number of arty businesses taking advantage of the cheap rent. You may have to wait in line for the city's most popular ramen (see pg 120), but don't despair: the queue moves fast, and the wait is worth it. Speaking of quality eats, Anderson Road is popping with 'em: you'll find everything from Thai to gourmet burgers on this long stretch, as well as one of Austin's most beloved toy stores (see pg 122).

1   Bicycle Sport Shop (off map)
2   Hopdoddy Burger Bar
3   Noble Sandwich Co. (off map)
4   Pinballz Arcade
5   Ramen Tatsu-Ya
6   Tâm Deli & Cafe
7   Terra Toys
8   The Goodnight
9   Tomodachi Sushi (off map)
10   Travaasa Austin (off map)

BICYCLE SPORT SHOP

Two-wheeler rental

10947 Research Boulevard (78759) / +1 512 345 7460
bicyclesportshop.com / Open daily

Thanks to one of our most famous/infamous residents, Lance Armstrong, Austin has a thriving bike culture – and Bicycle Sport Shop is the go-to place for cyclists to buy or rent equipment. But you don't have to be semi-pro to walk away with a lovely machine: BSS boasts three locations in Austin, with friendly staff at each post to help you find exactly what you want. On top of that, there are weekly group rides that guide you along some of the best road routes and mountain bike trails, or BSS will provide you with maps (along with helmet and pedals of your choice) for your own exploring. So hop on a bike and get out there!

HOPDODDY BURGER BAR

Ridiculously good hamburgers

2438 West Anderson Lane (78757) / +1 512 467 2337 / hopdoddy.com
Open daily

Hopdoddy's two locations in town both command long lines, so I'm
telling you about this one because the wait here is a bit shorter. These
are hamburgers for grown-ups who appreciate a more culinary filling in
their buns than a plain beef patty. Try the Angus beef topped with goat
cheese and basil pesto, or sushi-grade ahi tuna with pickled ginger and
honey wasabi. Buns are made fresh twice a day, the beef is hormone- and
antibiotic-free, and tasty meats including bison and lamb also make the
menu. If at all possible, finish off with a Nutella and chocolate pretzel
shake. A little selective gluttony won't hurt you.

NOBLE SANDWICH CO.

Not your everyday sarnie

Ste 105 12233 North 620 (78750) / +1 512 382 6248
noblesandwiches.com / Open daily

Sandwiches are typically the old workhorse of lunchtime everywhere –
a turkey/cheese packed in your sack, a roast beef sub on the run – but
at Noble Sandwich Co., where absolutely everything but the chips and
mayo are homemade, they're an immersive culinary experience in and of
themselves. I've never liked that reject of the dairy case, pimento cheese,
until, that is, I tried Noble's version. Piled thick on rye bread with crunchy
bacon, smoked green onions and house pickles providing the perfect
"ting!" inside all that richness, this sandwich demands your time and
attention – which after one bite, you are all too happy to give.

PINBALLZ ARCADE

Old-school gaming

8940 Research Boulevard (78758) / +1 512 420 8458
pinballzarcade.com / Open daily

In a world of technological ubiquity and digitized everything, it's refreshing to find an old school arcade such as Pinballz. The gigantic 13,000-square-foot game hall offers wall-to-wall amusements dating back generations, with skeeball (you can't resist skeeball), '80s/'90s video games and whirring, dinging pinball cases everywhere you look. Played the old fashioned way, with tokens and tickets, there are sweet prizes available too – but the best one? The triumphant, fist-pumping glory of finally beating Donkey Kong.

RAMEN TATSU-YA

Jaw-dropping, soul-warming ramen

8557 Research Boulevard (78758) / +1 512 339 0855
ramen-tatsuya.com / Closed Monday

In an unlikely corner of Austin, there lies a ramen noodle house named among *Bon Appétit*'s Top 50 New Restaurants within a year of opening. The crowds who flock here and the media both point to an essential truth about Ramen Tatsu-Ya: food this sumptuous is extremely rare. Their signature dish, the Tonkotsu Original, is a precise science of preparation, starting with a creamy emulsion of pork bone broth that's best eaten within 20 minutes according to the owners. Japanese soul food at its damned finest, the rest of the menu is fantastic as well — even the citrusy, relatively simple spicy edamame is a treat — but if it's your first time, go for ramen. The 20-minute rule will be no problem.

TÂM DELI & CAFE

The key to bánh mì

8222 North Lamar Boulevard (78753) / +1 512 834 6458
facebook.com/tamdeliandcafe / Closed Tuesday

Like Clark Kent, Tâm Deli & Cafe is somewhat unassuming to the naked eye. But also like Clark Kent, it doesn't take much to rip off the wrappings and reveal the power within – and by "much", I mean less than eight dollars. A beloved Vietnamese eatery run by two sisters, Tâm and Tran, Tâm Deli is famous for its bánh mì: think warm French bread enveloping a salad-like parcel of pickled carrots, jalapeños, fresh cilantro, cucumbers and juicy lemongrass beef. Polish it off with a petite cream puff, crisped and fried on the outside with custard-like goodness within.

TERRA TOYS

Wonder-filled children's store

2438 West Anderson Lane (78757) / +1 512 445 4489 / terratoys.com
Open daily

The first thing you notice at Terra Toys is the color exploding from the walls, from the stenciled, hand-painted stairs to the character etched into every toy. The second thing you'll notice is that it's easy to get lost inside each secret compartment here, such as the "pranks" wall (fake cockroaches, spiders and other creepy crawlies) or the library that's filled with old storybooks and a thousand plush toys. But the part I could spend hours in? The dollhouse section. From miniature beds to tiny rugs, Victorian housemaids to gadget-connected hipsters, it's an irresistible world to enter — a world that measures just a few feet wide.

THE GOODNIGHT

Bowling, booze and stellar eats

2700 West Anderson Lane (78757) / +1 512 459 5000
thegoodnightaustin.com / Open daily

A modern games lounge, vintage bowling alley and bar/restaurant,
The Goodnight packs in a lot of fun all at once. Go on a weekday when
it's slightly less crowded, and you can also take advantage of seven-dollar
pizzas – one of my favorites on the fancy bar food menu. Chef Danny
Bressler, who cut his teeth at South Congress Cafe (see pg 69) and Frank,
cooks from scratch and tops the Margherita pizza with a generous amount
of shredded basil and garlic confit: two ingredients that might not guarantee
you kisses, but then your mouth will be so happy, it won't need them.

TOMODACHI SUSHI

Worth-the-drive Japanese

4101 West Parmer Lane (78727) / +1 512 821 9472
tomosushiaustin.com / Closed Sunday

Tomodachi is a little off the beaten path, but the trek here is more than worth it. A Japanese house with sleek lines and tanks of glowing blue jellyfish greeting you at the door, Tomodachi almost feels formal, but as soon as you see menu items such as "Who's Ur Daddy", "Ex-Girlfriend" and "Say My Name!", you know you're in for some fun. Chef Steve Diad came to Austin from Las Vegas' famed Nobu, and playfulness is as important to him as precision. Sushi and sashimi are perfectly turned out, while American-styled dishes incorporate ingredients like mozzarella, jalapeño and spicy mayo. This is a serious kitchen with exuberant dishes, so enjoy yourself here – and don't be surprised if you make the trek again next week.

TRAVAASA AUSTIN

A beautifying, spiritual getaway

13500 Farm to Market Road 2769 (78726) / +1 877 261 7792
travaasa.com/austin / Open daily

To get to Travaasa Austin, you must first pass through a tree-lined tunnel on an old country road, which looks as though it's taking you to the middle of nowhere. In fact, it's weaving you through the Balcones Canyonlands Preserve, where Travaasa sits on a hilltop, nestled in thick forest and ancient rock. I've had many treatments at the spa, from facials to watsu baths, and they are all fantastic — but the spiritual serenity of the place alone is worth the sojourn. At night the sky is combed through with stars, and the voices of hill country creatures call out, welcoming your wild self back home.

ELEPHANT ROOM
315 Congress Avenue (78701), +1 512 473 2279, elephantroom.com
open daily

MOHAWK
912 Red River Street (78701), +1 512 666 0877, mohawkaustin.com
open daily

STUBB'S BAR-B-Q
801 Red River Street (78701), +1 512 480 8341, stubbsaustin.com
open daily

THE CACTUS CAFÉ & BAR
2247 Guadalupe Street (78712), +1 512 475 6515, cactuscafe.org
closed Sunday

THE CONTINENTAL CLUB
1315 South Congress Avenue (78704), +1 512 441 2444
continentalclub.com/Austin, open daily

THE HOLE IN THE WALL
2538 Guadalupe Street (78705), +1 512 302 1470
holeinthewallaustin.com, open daily

THE SAXON PUB
1320 South Lamar Boulevard (78704), +1 512 448 2552
thesaxonpub.com, open daily

WATERLOO RECORDS
600A North Lamar Boulevard (78703), +1 512 474 2500
waterloorecords.com, open daily

STUBB'S BAR-B-Q

On any given night, you can wander down the streets of Austin and hear live bands wailing through the doorways. Music purveyors and appreciators exist on such a wide spectrum here that come nightfall, you can usually find something to suit your precise taste and mood – though I find I'm pretty much always in the mood for **Elephant Room**, a literally underground jazz club on Congress Avenue. Once upon a time it fizzed with smoke and airbrushed drums; the drums are still there, and though a ban wiped out all the cigarettes, there's still a smoky sensuality in the air.

Stubb's Bar-B-Q is nearby on Red River, and its national-act-attracting outdoor amphitheater is glorious on a cool spring night. Also on Red River, you'll find a rowdy bastion of rock and indie music with the occasional sprinkling of live hip hop; that would be **Mohawk**, whose crowd skews a little younger and ironic T-shirt-wearing, and whose viewing setup is one of my favorites: there's a wrap-around upstairs balcony that doubles the audience.

Up near the UT campus, you've got two classic Austin options for live tunes: a ramshackle, wonderful bar called **The Hole in the Wall**, where the kick drum can be heard from the street and the bathrooms are covered in graffiti, and **The Cactus Café & Bar**, whose red curtains and classy round tables lend themselves well to the performers coming through (heartfelt singer songwriters and sophisticate country crooners).

Head south and stop in at **Waterloo Records**, either for a long, leisurely browse through their music stacks, or to catch an in-store performance from somebody famous: just know that the intimate confines of the store make these shows ticket-competitive, so buy early.

Once you've crossed the river, swing into **The Continental Club** on South Congress: rich musical history reverberates from the walls, along with the lively rockabilly and blues bands on stage. And finally, for more of a "listening library" experience, step into **The Saxon Pub**, a regular stop for both regional and local legends thanks to its hushed crowd and superior acoustics.

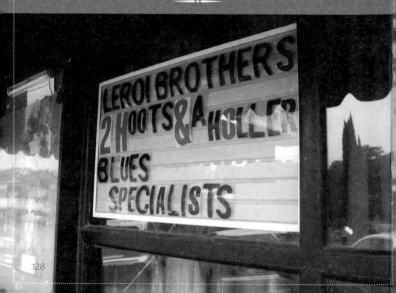